Miami Magic

Rich Hebron

Miami Magic

Rich Hebron

Books by Rich Hebron

Homeless but Human
Primary Ponderings

Nuance & Notes Series

Chicago Clarity
Paris Beauty
New York Energy
Los Angeles Dreams
Miami Magic
Milwaukee Sensibility
Mexico City Merriness
London Happening

Written by Rich Hebron
Illustrated by Kenneth Ferguson

Milly Moves to the Farm
The Boy and the Rocketship

Rich Edition Classics

The Great Gatsby

Rich Hebron is an American author. He has lived half his life in Chicago and the other half on a farm in rural Wisconsin. He fuses these backgrounds together to draw inspiration and live a meaningful life in a world accelerated by the internet and digital technology. He hosts the Rich Conversations Podcast where he explores self-development and talks with friends in art and science fields.

Connect with Rich: @richhebron

For those who want to create magic

Author's Note

My first near-death experience happened on the farm. An oil line blew on the tractor and became engulfed in flames. I jumped from it. My second near-death experience occurred four years afterwards. This time, three men pointed Uzi guns at my face, threatening to shoot me. Fortunately, it was just another reminder that life will end—all our lives. So how do we want ours to be?

After initially going fast, with the adrenaline from the encounter lasting months, I decided to stop. The difference between speed and velocity is that velocity is speed in a direction. Anyone can go fast—especially in circles. But it takes skill and something deeper to channel energy with purpose. Refining purpose requires restarting at the beginning. Be open and see what's happening. Pursue curiosity and, above all, patience.

My curiosity led me to hotel lobbies. I spent time visiting different ones in downtown Chicago and just sat, observed, and wrote notes, often sipping espresso or red wine. An appreciation for details developed. Gratitude followed. Every thing was there for a reason. Nothing was a coincidence. The creators of the spaces aimed to evoke particular emotions and feelings in people. They staged a vibe.

I learned that design affects our mind and influences our culture. The whole of something is the result of individual things. From a pencil to a house. From a shoe to our cities. From a light fixture to our lives. The story of our life is the result of every individual decision we make. The universe is the result of every individual atom.

Beauty is the result of those small, individual components. Love is understanding those small, individual components.

My passion and appreciation for detail expanded from hotel lobbies to virtually everything in life and in people. But something I especially had fun with was observing the designs on building facades. My favorites were those resembling nature. They possessed the character I aspire to be: dynamic, flexible, playful, and fruitful. Things that are alive are adaptable. Things that are dead are stiff, rigid, and brittle. Since human beings are part of nature, the same is true for people and their ideas and perspectives.

I encourage you to reflect on the follow questions:

- *Are current environments failing to design nuance?*
- *If design affects culture, what are the ramifications of prioritizing cheap and fast?*
- *Is a society that ignores patience a healthy one?*
- *If individuality is abandoned, is Love too?*

This is a series called *Nuance & Notes*.
This is a book of nuance of Miami with notes from my mind and observations in the world.

Step foot in Miami, take a breath, and feel the body heal. It's an invigorating and inspiring place. The sun and ocean brings the city to life and creates a unique and regenerative spirit. People say "good morning" to each other because it is and can be. Half the work is already done to make it a beautiful day. Miami feels the least and most like America. Its Latin influence and multicultural setting mixes with the embodied beliefs that dreams are within reach. Above all, Miami knows how to have fun and celebrate life. The city is indeed magic.

Shot on iPhone 13 Mini

Magic is awesome

Rich Hebron

Sometimes we have to hit a wall
before we can find the door

Be alive

It only takes one breath to be revitalized

What would refresh our thoughts?

Rich Hebron

Celebrate the abundance of life

Whenever feeling sluggish,
imagine a disco ball above a pool
surrounded by palm trees

Don't take our senses for granted
Pause and breathe in
What information can be absorbed?

Something is always happening
Do we see it?

Live a life full of color

Walk on the beach
with our feet in the water
and lose track of time

Observe the spectrum of colors
with appreciation

Let the energy flow through us
and move our body in rhythm

We're free
Breathe
Smile

Be silent and let the sounds inspire us

Rich Hebron

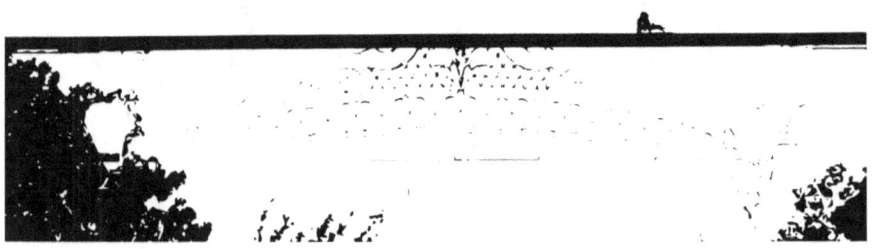

Can we live without
constantly knowing the time?

We'll never be younger
than we are in this moment

The ability to flow in the world
is not something to ignore

When we're here,
be here

Feel the energy of life around us

Our imagination is as bright as the Sun

A walk on a warm humid night is magical

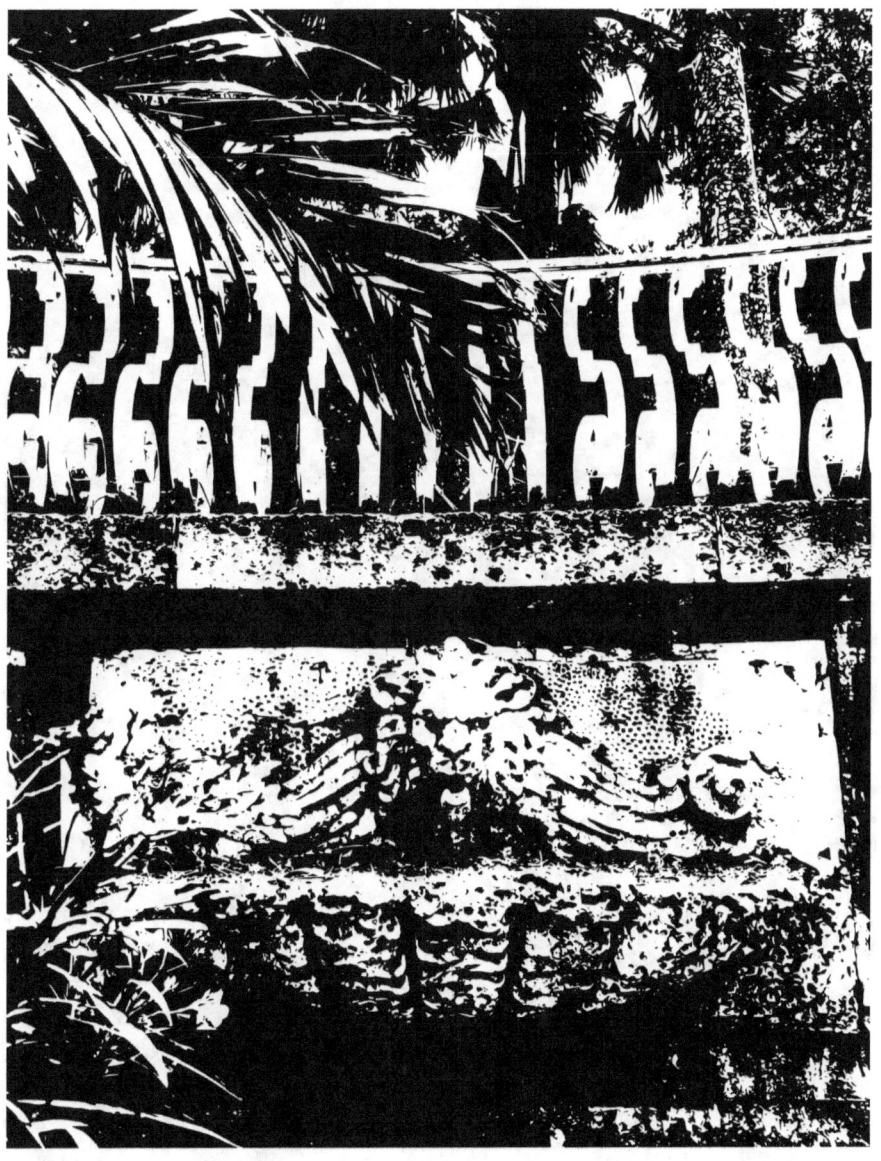

Say good morning to others
It's small but it elevates the collective

Rich Hebron

The biggest difference
is between a sick and a well person

Nurture our friendships
so they bloom like flowers

Rich Hebron

Those who can't see, fight
Those who can see, dance

Lead with our energy and effort

We can do anything with magic

Remember always
that we can't get time back
Remember this always

What we choose to do in a day reveals much

Playing the game of life requires
objective perspective of the cards
and strengths we possess

Rich Hebron

Step with lightness
like we're on our way to a festival

We do what we do for the opportunity
to experience absolute bliss

Rich Hebron

We can live with mistakes
We cannot live with regrets

The more universal,
the more impactful and long lasting

Rich Hebron

If our journey looks like a straight line,
it is likely be boring
and full of regret

What do we find easy
that others find hard?

A place with elevated vibrations
is a magical place

Life is an amalgamation
of past decisions

Originality is being
and the world is starved for it

If one aspect is off,
all aspects are off

Rich Hebron

Visualize what will electrify

How flexible is our life right now?
Can we adapt and flow
with what comes our way?

Rich Hebron

There's spirit here

We never know when our light will go out,
so shine bright

When we think back
to our favorite moments in life,
what repeats?

See the big picture
and put less weight
on individual experience

What have we been too comfortable to do?

Spend time in places
where people say good morning

Identify sources of illness and heal them

Travel light and flow with what happens

Do today what will make it a great day
Repeat that process again the next day
and the days forward

If we want to change our future,
start by observing
our past habits, actions, and results

Rich Hebron

Time spent in the presence
or in conversation with a friend
is always worthwhile

The intersection of fulfillment
arises from purpose and talent

Rich Hebron

Take a step back
What're some blessings around us?

The spirit is contagious here

The sun shines bright and gives its energy
Step into the light and awaken our self

What if we've been thinking too small?

Life is more enriching
with variety and flavors

Ask and wait
Proceed with the instructions

Rich Hebron

Our horizon expands in relation
to our openness to unknown things

It's hard to score if we don't attempt
It's impossible to win if we don't score

If the table is set,
not showing up for dinner would be rude

Live our life with passion
and give compassion to others

The sun makes a difference with people
But if the sun isn't out,
let our light shine regardless

What's something we do
that makes time disappear like magic?

Beautiful things are happening
all the time

Fear is not even trying
because the results might not be
what we desire

Appreciate areas of the world
where life thrives

Be where we love to be

Rich Hebron

Palm trees are inspiring

Be present enough
to be impressed with flamingos

Jealousy is a silly thing
if we step back and observe

Fresh air is magic

Do our most important work of the day
when we have our greatest energy and focus

If we want more connection,
we must be the source of energy

Rich Hebron

When we work together,
we'll make the world believe in magic

When things get tough,
that's when life gets interesting
That's when character is revealed

Rich Hebron

Celebrate a life of color and brightness

When we look back,
we'll have the biggest smile on our face
Live like that

The dots can only be connected
forward not backwards

Be invigorated by the bright

Patience changes the game we play

Meet our expectations

Rich Hebron

Happiness is the effect of balance
Unhappiness is caused by imbalance

Something can only be divided if it believes
one interest is greater than all other interests

Rich Hebron

Sit by the ocean and just breathe

Whatever brings joy,
make time for in our life

This seashell went on our journey
to end up in our hand

A conversation with a friend
can wash away redundant thoughts
like ocean waves upon a beach

The moment we accept patience
is the moment our burden
becomes light

If experiencing pain,
try switching environments

Rich Hebron

Where we are is the result
of our past actions

Being outside in warm weather
is healthier than being
in front of a computer screen

Rich Hebron

Blow a kiss into the warm air

Some things will take time
and it won't do us good
to rush or get anxious

Where have we put most our energy lately?
Do the results fulfill us?

Where are we most reluctant?
Why do we feel this way?
How can we flow better?

An iguana may approach us
Just be cool

We assign with our mind
whether something is big or small

Some people focus on lyrics
Some people focus on sound

Would we rather swim in
an empty ocean or a crowded pool?

Nurture our relationships with friends so
they're always giving us life

The optimistic find reasons to party

Move our body while we can

No job is too small,
especially when it ensures
the safety of another

Rich Hebron

If we reduce our ego,
we learn more today than we did yesterday

It's hard to feel lonely
when a peacock is nearby watching us

Rich Hebron

Stare at each sunset
because we never know if it's our last

Something seems big
but when we do it
that something becomes small

We can do more if we work together and
share our resources, talents, and skills

Exercise being happy in this moment

Our worst enemy is often
our expectations and attachments

What is demanded but not oversaturated?
Therein lies opportunity

Love wherever we are in life
It's part of our journey

The weight of a thing is significant,
both when heavy or light

We can smell the ocean even from afar

Celebrate living and smile about it

Rich Hebron

Demonstrate composure

Breathe in the warm breeze

Make wherever we are magical

What's the greatest source of our energy?
Give attention to that

Live a life of abundant celebrations

When we surpass
our visualized limit,
it's magical

Let the vibrations and energy lead the dance

We're here
Let's have fun

A Thought on Cities

Our cities are our greatest invention. They're the engines of civilization. Cities are the hubs that bring people, ideas, and opportunities together. They generate energy and inspire the pursuit of dreams and a better life.

I feel humans are meant to be isolated in nature or surrounded by other humans. Fusing the two maximizes energy and accelerates regenerative processes. This is why I shuffle between living on a farm in rural America and traveling to big international cities.

Having lived in Chicago for over 15 years, I am an enthusiastic advocate for urban living. I believe that the healthier the city, the more dynamic the society and culture. I'm passionate about exploring and analyzing the facets of each city. I believe in competition and that our cities should be constantly learning, adapting, evolving, and growing to serve and increase the quality of life for its residents. I love observing and comparing cities, noting their strengths and weaknesses, the effects of local geography, the movements and flows, and how every small matter contributes to the larger matter.

Cities are where big things happen. I believed this as a little kid growing up on a farm and I know it now as an adult who has experienced their impact.

I'm proud to combine notes that can help realize individual human potential with artwork that demonstrates the beauty collaboration can produce.

Rich leads weekly self-reflection sessions
to help people create magic in their lives

Join in on the Rich Conversations Podcast
or visit the Rich Hebron YouTube channel

Connect with Rich: @richhebron

Notes

Notes

Notes

Notes

www.ingramcontent.com/pod-product-compliance
Lightning Source LLC
Chambersburg PA
CBHW071758120626
46550CB00002B/835